Alfred's

# Music for Little Mozarts

## Meet the Music Friends

### 5 Introductory Music Lessons for Ages 4–6

Alfred
IQ

## Christine H. Barden · Gayle Kowalchyk · E. L. Lancaster

# Contents

Alfred Music Publishing Co., Inc.
P.O. Box 10003
Van Nuys, CA 91410-0003
**alfred.com**

ISBN-10: 0-7390-8112-8
ISBN-13: 978-0-7390-8112-9

Cover art by Christine Finn

# Preliminary Information

## About Meet the Music Friends

*Meet the Music Friends* was written to provide an introduction to music and the piano for four- and five-year olds. It consists of a series of five lessons that include singing, listening, movement, rhythm activities, and beginning activities at the keyboard. The lessons center around the adventures of Beethoven Bear and Mozart Mouse, characters who live in the piano classroom of a music store, as they learn about music. After completing the five lessons, students should begin Level 1 of the *Music for Little Mozarts* piano course.

## To The Teacher

*Meet the Music Friends* was designed to be taught in a music classroom with one keyboard instrument. Other materials needed to teach the five lessons are:

Curriculum Book with CD (37545)

Music Workbook for each student (37548)

Beethoven Bear Plush Animal (14654)

Mozart Mouse Plush Animal (14653)

Clara Schumann-Cat Plush Animal (19767)

CD Player

Crayons for each student

The Curriculum Book contains complete lesson plans for a classroom lesson of 45-60 minutes. Each lesson plan consists of three parts: 1) a list of teaching materials needed for the lesson; 2) a lesson overview – a brief summary of what is included in the lesson; 3) a detailed lesson plan, including step-by-step instructions for teaching the curriculum. When first teaching the curriculum, most teachers will want to follow the detailed lesson plan. After having taught the course a few times, teachers can easily follow the lesson overview.

The authors hope that you and your students enjoy your musical adventures with your music friends, Beethoven Bear and Mozart Mouse.

## CD Track List

| Track | Title |
| --- | --- |
| 1 | Hello Song |
| 2 | High and Low Song |
| 3 | The Itsy Bitsy Spider |
| 4 | Johnny Works with One Hammer |
| 5 | Goodbye Song |
| 6 | Mozart Mouse's Song |
| 7 | If You're Happy and You Know It |
| 8 | Beethoven Bear's Song |
| 9 | The Old Gray Cat |
| 10 | The Whole Note Song |

# Lesson 1
## Meet the Music Friends

**Musical Concept Emphasis: High and Low, Up and Down, Steady Beat**

## Teaching Materials

- ❑ *Meet the Music Friends* Curriculum Book and CD
- ❑ *Meet the Music Friends* Music Workbook for each student (pages 2-3)
- ❑ CD player
- ❑ Beethoven Bear and Mozart Mouse plush animals
- ❑ Crayons for each student

page 2

page 3

## Lesson 2 Overview

### Part 1: Hello Song
- *Hello Song* (💿 1)

### Part 2: Beethoven Bear and Mozart Mouse
- Show Beethoven Bear and Mozart Mouse Plush Animals.
- Read story.

### Part 3: High and Low
- *High and Low Song* (💿 2)
- Demonstrate high and low sounds on keyboard.
- Complete Music Workbook, pages 2-3.

### Part 4: Up and Down
- *The Itsy Bitsy Spider* (💿 3)
- Demonstrate sounds that go up and down on the keyboard.

### Part 5: Steady Beat
- *Johnny Works with One Hammer* (💿 4)

### Part 6: Goodbye Song
- *Goodbye Song* (💿 5)

## Part 1: Hello Song

| Teacher | Students |
|---|---|
| 1. Begin class by playing *Hello Song* (🎧 **1**).  As the song plays, demonstrate the movements in the lyrics:  wave hello, clap hands, stamp feet, turn around, touch the ground. | 1. Stand and imitate motions. |
| 2. Say:  "This song is about two music friends who will be visiting our class today.  Listen to the *Hello Song* again to learn their names." | |
| 3. *Play Hello* Song again.  Encourage the children to do the motions and sing the lyrics. | |

## Part 2: Beethoven Bear and Mozart Mouse

| Teacher | Children |
|---|---|
| 1. Say, "We sang about our new music friends, Beethoven Bear and Mozart Mouse. Tell me their names as you see me hold up each one." <br><br> [Beethoven Bear and Mozart Mouse] <br><br> 2. Say: "Today we have a story about Beethoven Bear and Mozart Mouse. Listen carefully to find out where they live and what they like to do." <br><br> 3. Read the story aloud. | 1. Sit, listen, and answer questions. |

# Chapter 1: Beethoven Bear and Mozart Mouse and the Musical Question

Once upon a time, there was a music store where children just about your age came for music lessons. In that store, there was a special room for piano lessons. It had colorful posters on the walls, shelves filled with books and music, baskets of crayons and markers and even a white board with magnets and colored markers. But the most wonderful thing in the room was the piano. And sitting on the piano were a little stuffed bear and a little stuffed mouse. Their names were Beethoven Bear and Mozart Mouse.

The little animals loved the children who came to take piano lessons! All day long, Beethoven Bear and Mozart Mouse would sit quietly on the piano, letting the children play with them and move them around during their lessons. But at night, it was a different story. As soon as the last lesson was finished, and everyone had left the music store, Beethoven Bear and Mozart Mouse would turn on the lights and practice the piano! You see, they listened very carefully during the children's lessons because they wanted to play, too.

One night while they were practicing, Beethoven Bear asked Mozart Mouse a very interesting question. "Which sounds do you like better – the high sounds or the low sounds?"

Mozart Mouse said without hesitation, "I like high sounds the best! Which ones do you like?"

Beethoven Bear replied, "I like low sounds the best. They are perfect for a bear like me."

"And I think high sounds are perfect for a mouse like me," Mozart Mouse said.

And so went the conversation that Beethoven Bear and Mozart Mouse had many times when they practiced the piano. Each night, they would take out the books that the teacher always used at the lessons. "These are very special books," Beethoven Bear said. Mozart Mouse agreed. "The children learn so many wonderful things from them." They spent many happy hours playing the piano.

You, too, can learn many wonderful things about music and the piano in our class. Beethoven Bear and Mozart Mouse want you to join in their musical adventures. They are our new music friends and together, they will take us on a journey through the exciting world of music.

| Teacher | Children |
|---|---|
| 4. Ask: "Where do Beethoven Bear and Mozart Mouse live?" <br><br> [in the piano classroom of a music store] | 4. Sit and answer question. |

## Part 3: High and Low

| Teacher | Students |
|---|---|
| 1. Ask: "Who likes the low sounds best?"<br><br>[Beethoven Bear]<br><br>Ask: "Who likes the high sounds best?"<br><br>[Mozart Mouse] | 1. Sit and answer questions. |
| 2. Say: "Our music friends have a special song about high and low. Everyone please stand. When we hear the high sounds that Mozart Mouse likes, we are going to stretch up high. When we hear the low sounds that Beethoven Bear likes, we are going to bend down low."<br><br>• Sing *High and Low Song* (💿2) | 2. Stand, sing, stretch up for high sounds, and bend down for low sounds. |

| Teacher | Students |
|---|---|
| 3. Say: "Let's see what high and low sounds are like on the piano."<br><br>   • Demonstrate high and low sounds on the piano. | 3. Gather around piano and identify high and low sounds. |

Low Sounds

High Sounds

• Optional: Students take turns playing high and low sounds on the piano.

Optional: Take turns playing high and low sounds.

• Ask the students to close their eyes. Play a high sound or a low sound. Ask a student to place Beethoven Bear or Mozart Mouse in the correct place on the keyboard. Repeat until everyone has had a turn.

Low Sounds              High Sounds

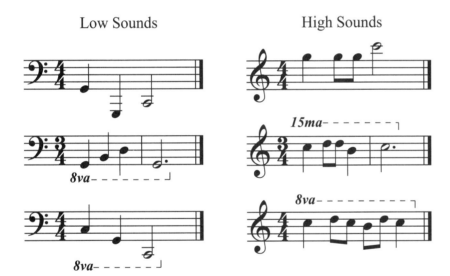

4. Say: "Please sit down. We have special books like the ones in the story. When I give you a book, please turn to pages 2 and 3 with the pictures of Beethoven Bear and Mozart Mouse standing on the keys." Hold up the pages for them to see.

4. Sit on floor and open Music Workbook to pages 2 and 3.

5. Ask: "Which music friend is standing near the low sounds?"

[Beethoven Bear]

"Which music friend is standing near the high sounds?"

[Mozart Mouse]

• Color the pictures as instructed in the Music Workbook.

5. Answer questions and color pages 2 and 3 in Music Workbook.

# Part 4: Up and Down

| Teacher | Students |
|---|---|
| 1. Say: "We know that music can sound high or low. Music can also go up and down." | 1. Stand, sing, and imitate motions. |
| 2. Ask: "Who knows the song about *The Itsy Bitsy Spider*? It sounds like this. (Demonstrate the first few lines of the song.) In the song, the spider goes up the waterspout and then back down. Let's stand and sing the song and do the motions." | |
| • Play *The Itsy Bitsy Spider* (💿 3). Sing and do the motions. | |

| Teacher | Students |
|---|---|
| 3. Say: "Listen to what sounds going up and sounds going down are like on the piano." | 3. Gather around piano and identify sounds that move up and down. |

- Demonstrate up and down sounds.

Sounds that move up

Sounds that move down

- Optional: Students take turns playing up and down sounds on the piano.

Optional: Take turns playing up and down sounds on the keyboard.

- Ask the students to close their eyes. Play up or down sounds. Ask a student to place Mozart Mouse high on the keyboard if the sounds go up. Ask a student to place Beethoven Bear low on the keyboard if the sounds go down. Repeat until everyone has a turn.

Sounds that move up

Sounds that move down

## Part 5: Steady Beat

| Teacher | Students |
|---|---|
| 1. Ask: "Have you ever tried to build something?  What kinds of tools did you use?  Usually we need a hammer to build things.  Let's sit and pretend we are hammering." | 1. Stand, sing, hammer with fists, and add motions to song. |
| • Make two fists and tap one on top of the other. | |
| 2. Say: "You are great with your hammers!  I bet you can hammer while we listen to some music.  Watch me.  There are some other motions for us to add." | |
| • Play *Johnny Works With One Hammer* (🎵4).  Add motions and sing. | |

**Johnny Works with One Hammer**

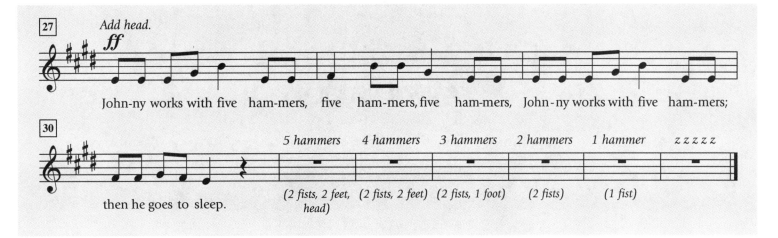

**27** *Add head.* *ff*

John-ny works with five ham-mers, five ham-mers, five ham-mers, John-ny works with five ham-mers;

**30**

| | 5 hammers | 4 hammers | 3 hammers | 2 hammers | 1 hammer | z z z z z |

then he goes to sleep. *(2 fists, 2 feet, head)* *(2 fists, 2 feet)* *(2 fists, 1 foot)* *(2 fists)* *(1 fist)*

3. Say: "Our hammers were nice and steady. In music, this is called a beat. We were making a steady beat when we were hammering with our fists."

## Part 6: Goodbye Song

| Teacher | Students |
|---|---|
| 1. Say: "You have all worked really hard today! We met our new music friends, Beethoven Bear and Mozart Mouse. We learned high and low and up and down on the keyboard. We know how to keep a steady beat. But now our time is over, and we have to say goodbye to our music friends. They have a special song to sing at the end of class. Stand and listen to it." | 1. Stand, sing, and imitate motions. |
| • Play *Goodbye Song* (🎧5). As the song plays, demonstrate the movements in the lyrics: take a bow, take a rest, wave goodbye. | |

**Goodbye Song**

*Peacefully* (♩ = 72) *mp*

It's time to say good-bye. It's

**3** *rit.* *a tempo*

time to take a bow. We tried our ve-ry best and now it's time to take a rest. It's

**6** *rit.*

time to say good-bye. Good-bye, good-bye, good-bye.

# Lesson 2
## Keyboard Concepts

Musical Concept Emphasis: Finger Numbers, Two- and Three-Black-Key Groups

## Teaching Materials

- ❑ *Meet the Music Friends* Curriculum Book and CD
- ❑ *Meet the Music Friends* Music Workbook for each student (pages 4–8)
- ❑ CD player

- ❑ Beethoven Bear, Mozart Mouse, and Clara Schumann-Cat plush animals
- ❑ Crayons for each student

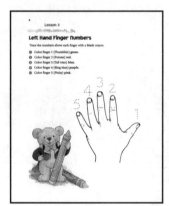

page 4

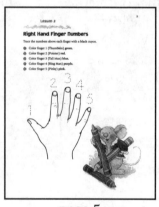

page 5

page 6

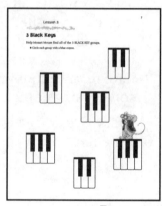

page 7

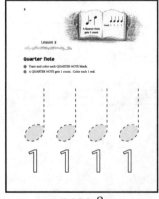

page 8

Note: Students can begin Music Workbook pages in the lesson and complete them at home.

## Lesson 2 Overview

**Part 1:  Hello Song and Review**

- *Hello Song* (💿 **1**)
- High and low sounds on keyboard

**Part 2:  Finger Numbers**

- Introduce finger numbers.
- Complete Music Workbook, pages 4–5.

**Part 3:  Twos and Threes**

- Read story.

**Part 4:  Two- and Three-Black Keys**

- Find and play groups of two black keys on the keyboard.

- Find and play groups of three black keys on the keyboard.
- Complete Music Workbook, pages 6–7.

**Part 5:  Review Steady Beat**

- *Johnny Works with One Hammer* (💿 **4**)
- *Mozart Mouse's Song* (💿 **6**)
- Introduce quarter notes.
- Complete Music Workbook, page 8.

**Part 6:  Goodbye Song**

- *Goodbye Song* (💿 **5**)

## Detailed Lesson Plan

### Part 1:  Hello Song and Review

| Teacher | Students |
|---|---|
| 1.  Sing *Hello Song* (💿 **1**) with the movements.  (See page 5 for lyrics.) | 1.  Stand, sing, and follow the teacher's movements. |
| 2.  Ask:  "What are the names of our music friends who like high and low sounds?"  [Beethoven Bear and Mozart Mouse]  Show Beethoven Bear and Mozart Mouse plush animals. | 2.  Sit and answer questions. |
| 3.  Ask:  "Who likes high sounds?"  [Mozart Mouse] | |
| 4.  Ask:  "Who likes low sounds?"  [Beethoven Bear] | |
| 5.  Say:  "Listen to some high and low sounds on the piano.  If you hear a high sound, raise your hand.  Then, we will put Mozart Mouse high on the keyboard.  If you hear a low sound, keep your hands in your lap.  Then, we will put Beethoven Bear low on the keyboard."  (See page 9 for examples of high and low sounds.) | 5.  Listen and respond accordingly. |

## Part 2: Finger Numbers

| Teacher | Students |
|---|---|
| 1. Say: "For playing the piano, we give each finger a number. Hold up both hands, spread out your fingers, and copy me. The thumb is the first finger in each hand. Wiggle your thumbs." | 1. Hold up hands and wiggle thumbs. |
| 2. Say: "Once we know where finger 1 is, then we can number the rest of our fingers. Put your hands in the air and show me fingers 2, 3, 4 and 5." (Turn back to class, raise hands in the air and wiggle fingers. Look over shoulder to check students' fingers.)<br><br>Note: Teachers may want to refer to finger 1 as thumbkin, finger 2 as pointer, finger 3 as tall man, finger 4 as ring man, and finger 5 as pinky. | 2. Hold hands in the air and wiggle fingers requested by the teacher. |
| 3. Say: "Excellent! Take out your Music Workbook and turn to pages 4 and 5 with the pictures of the hands on them. We are going to color the fingers on these pages." | 3. Sit and color fingers on pages 4 and 5 according to the directions in the Music Workbook. |

## Part 3: Twos and Threes

| Teacher | Students |
|---|---|
| 1. Say: "Put your books away now. Our music friends, Beethoven Bear and Mozart Mouse are going to have some more musical adventures. Listen to find out what they are doing today." | 1. Sit and listen. |
| 2. Read the story aloud. | |

# Chapter 2: Twos and Threes

Mozart Mouse was a very particular mouse. He liked things to be "just so." Quite often, after the music store was closed and the piano teacher had gone home, he could be found straightening up the piano room and putting things away. It was just such a night when he made a very exciting discovery.

"Beethoven Bear!" he cried. "Come here!"

Beethoven Bear was sitting at the piano and had just noticed that there was an interesting pattern to the black and white keys. When he heard his friend call to him, he jumped off the bench and ran to the other side of the room. By the time he arrived, he was clearly out of breath. He plopped down on the floor.

"This better be important," he gasped.

"I think it is," Mozart Mouse replied. Then he pointed to the corner of the room. "Look," he whispered.

Beethoven Bear rubbed his eyes in disbelief. There, in the corner of the piano room was a rather large, white, fluffy cat! And she was staring right at them! (Show Clara Schumann-Cat plush animal.)

Mozart Mouse hid behind his friend. You see, he was allergic to cats, and he was afraid he would start to sneeze.

Beethoven Bear puffed out his chest, pretending to be brave. "Who…who are you?" he stammered.

The cat swished her tail and replied, "Why, I believe I should be asking you that question. Who are you, and why are you in my piano room?"

Mozart Mouse stepped out bravely from behind Beethoven Bear. "I am Mozart Mouse, and this is my friend, Beethoven Bear. We help the children who take piano lessons here," he said proudly. Then he continued cautiously, "Why is this room your piano room?"

The cat rose to her full height and puffed up her chest. "I am Clara-Schumann Cat. I have lived all of my life here in the music store, and it is my duty to guard it at night."

Beethoven Bear and Mozart Mouse were quite impressed. Beethoven Bear exclaimed, "You must know *so* much about music."

"Indeed I do," Clara purred.

Beethoven Bear jumped at the opportunity. "Do you know how to play the piano?" he asked excitedly.

"Of course," Clara continued purring.

Beethoven Bear couldn't believe his ears. "Then would you mind showing me something on the keyboard?"

Clara answered, "I would be delighted," and the three went over to the piano. "What is it you would like to know?" she asked.

Beethoven Bear cleared his throat. "Well, I noticed that the black keys look like they make a pattern."

Clara Schumann-Cat chuckled. "Yes, you see, the black keys are grouped together in twos and threes." She pointed to a group of two black keys and then a group of three black keys as she spoke.

"Oh," Mozart Mouse said. "That *is* easy! Now we can play our favorite sounds using two and three black key groups!"

The two music friends were very excited. Then Mozart Mouse had an idea.

"Could you show us some more things about the piano?" he asked.

Clara Schumann-Cat swished her tail and smiled. "I've always wanted to teach piano," she said. "You will be my very first students."

Beethoven Bear and Mozart Mouse looked at each other in disbelief. They were going to take piano lessons!

"Can we begin right now?" Mozart Mouse asked.

"Absolutely," Clara purred. And so, Mozart Mouse and Beethoven Bear began their very own piano adventure.

## Part 4: Two- and Three-Black Keys

| Teacher | Students |
|---|---|
| 1. Say: "Beethoven Bear and Mozart Mouse discovered that the piano keyboard has black keys that are arranged in groups of twos and threes. We can find the groups of two black keys on the piano, too." | 1. Gather around the piano and listen for instructions. |
| 2. Ask: "Who can find a group of two black keys? Raise your hand. When I call your name, you can show us a group of two black keys." (Continue until everyone has had a turn.) | 2. Raise hand and show group of two black keys. |
| 3. Say: "You did a great job finding the groups of two black keys. Let's help Beethoven Bear and Mozart Mouse find the groups of three black keys." | |
| 4. Ask: "Who can find a group of three black keys? Raise your hand. When I call your name, you can show us a group of three black keys." (Continue until everyone has had a turn.) | 4. Raise hand and show group of three black keys. |
| 5. Say: "Take out your Music Workbook and turn to page 6. What do you see on this page?" [Groups of two and three black keys] | 5. Sit, open Music Workbook to page 6, and answer questions. |
| 6. Say: "Take a red crayon and circle the two-black-key groups. Hold up your book when you are finished so that I can check it." | 6. Circle the two-black-key groups on page 6 and hold up book. |
| 7. Say: "Good! Look at page 7. Take a blue crayon and circle the three-black-key groups. Hold up your book when you are finished." | 7. Circle the three-black-key groups on page 7 and hold up book. |

## Part 5: Review Steady Beat

| Teacher | Students |
|---|---|
| 1. Ask: "Who remembers how to hammer? We take our fists and tap them together to hammer with a steady beat. I want to see how steady you can hammer to our song, *Johnny Works with One Hammer.*" (See page 12 for lyrics.)<br><br>• Play *Johnny Works with One Hammer* (🎵 **4**). | 1. Stand, sing, and hammer fists. |
| 2. Say: "We have another song with a steady beat. It's about our music friend, Mozart Mouse. Let's listen to it."<br><br>• Play *Mozart Mouse's Song* (🎵 **6**). | 2. Sit and listen. |

🎵 **6**

# Mozart Mouse's Song

Playfully ( ♩ = 120)

*mp*

Mo - zart Mouse said, "Oh, please,

will you sing a song with me? I have friends here to play. We will have a mu-sic day."

| Teacher | Students |
|---|---|
| 3. Say: "Now, we will clap a steady beat as we sing *Mozart Mouse's Song.*" | 3. Sing *Mozart Mouse's Song* and clap a steady beat. |
| 4. Say: "You are really good at keeping a steady beat! Take out your Music Workbook again. Turn to page 8. This is a quarter note. (Point to quarter note.) A quarter note gets one count. When we clap quarter notes, we keep a steady beat." Demonstrate clapping and counting some quarter notes. | 4. Open Music Workbook to page 8. |
| 5. Say: "Trace and color each quarter note with a black crayon. Then color each '1' with a red crayon." | 5. Color quarter notes black and "1" red on page 8. |
| 6. Say: "Now, clap and count the quarter notes." | 6. Clap and count, saying "1" for each quarter note. |

## Part 6: Goodbye Song

| Teacher | Students |
|---|---|
| 1. Say: "We worked really hard today and learned a lot! We met a new music friend, Clara Schumann-Cat and, she told Beethoven Bear and Mozart Mouse what the pattern of black keys is on the piano. You played groups of two and three black keys on the keyboard. And you learned about quarter notes. Our class is over for today, so we will sing the *Goodbye Song.*" (See page 13 for lyrics.)<br><br>• Play *Goodbye Song* (🌀 5). | 1. Stand, sing, and imitate motions. |

# Lesson 3
## Loud and Soft

Musical Concept Emphasis: Half Note, Loud and Soft

## Teaching Materials

❑ *Meet the Music Friends* Curriculum Book and CD

❑ *Meet the Music Friends* Music Workbook for each student (pages 9-11)

❑ CD player

❑ Beethoven Bear, Mozart Mouse, and Clara Schumann-Cat plush animals

❑ Crayons for each student

page 9

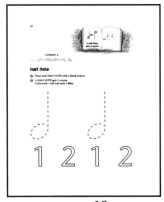

page 10

page 11

Note: Students can begin Music Workbook pages in the lesson and complete them at home.

## Lesson 3 Overview

### Part 1: Hello Song and Review Two- and Three-Black-Key Groups

- *Hello Song* (🎵 1)
- Review finger numbers.
- Review and play groups of two black keys.
- *If You're Happy and You Know It* (🎵 7)
- Review and play groups of three black keys.

### Part 2: Quarter Note Review

- *Mozart Mouse's Song* (🎵 6)
- Complete Music Workbook, page 9.

### Part 3: Loud and Soft

- Read story.

### Part 4: Half Notes, Loud and Soft Sounds

- *Beethoven Bear's Song* (🎵 8)
- Introduce half notes
- Complete Music Workbook, pages 10–11.

### Part 5: Goodbye Song

- *Goodbye Song* (🎵 5)

# Detailed Lesson Plan

## Part 1: Hello Song and Review Two- and Three-Black-Key Groups

| Teacher | Students |
|---|---|
| 1. Sing *Hello Song* (🎵 **1**) with the movements. (See page 5 for lyrics.) | 1. Stand, sing, and follow the teacher's movements. |
| 2. Say: "In our last class, we gave each of our fingers a number. I'll point to one of my fingers, and you tell me the number." (Hold hand up to class with back of hand facing children. Point to fingers and have the class say the number. Start with finger 1, then 2, then 3, etc., then mix them up.) | 2. Sit and name finger numbers. |
| 3. Say: "You remember the numbers really well! Put your hands together like this (show hands facing palm to palm and fingers touching). Follow me and tap your fingers together. Tap your thumbs, your 2s, your 3s, your 4s, your 5s, (continue and mix up finger numbers.)" | 3. Place hands together and tap fingers as instructed. |
| 4. Say: "Excellent! Come with me to the piano. We need to place Beethoven Bear and Mozart Mouse near their favorite sounds. I need someone to place Beethoven Bear near his favorite sounds." [Low] | 4. Gather around the piano. Place Beethoven Bear low on the keyboard. |
| 5. Say: "Great! Now I need someone to place Mozart Mouse near his favorite sounds." [High] | 5. Place Mozart Mouse high on the keyboard. |
| 6. Say: "Next, we are going to take fingers 2 and 3 on your left hand and play a group of two black keys." The two black keys in the group can be played either individually or simultaneously. Take turns until all students have played. | 6. Play a group of two black keys with left hand using fingers 2 and 3. |
| 7. Say: "Now, we are going to take fingers 2 and 3 on your right hand and play a group of two black keys." The two black keys in the group can be played either individually or simultaneously. Take turns until all students have played. | 7. Play a group of two black keys with right hand using fingers 2 and 3. |
| 8. Ask: "Who knows this song?"<br><br>• Play *If You're Happy and You Know It* (🎵 **7**) | 8. Listen, sing, and do motions. |

# If You're Happy and You Know It

1. If you're hap-py and you know it, clap your

hands! *(clap hands)* If you're hap-py and you know it, clap your

hands! *(clap hands)* If you're hap-py and you know it, then your

face will sure-ly show it, if you're hap-py and you know it, clap your hands! *(clap hands)*

2. stamp your feet *(stamp feet)*
3. jump up high *(jump high)*

4. do all three *(clap hands, stamp feet, jump high)*

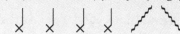

| Teacher | Students |
|---|---|
| 9. Say: "We are going to sing it again, but this time, we are going to change the words. Instead of singing, 'If you're happy and you know it, clap your hands,' we are going to sing, 'If you're happy and you know it, play two keys.' Then, you will play two black keys with fingers 2 and 3 with either hand (tap, tap)." (Sing and demonstrate.) | 9. Stand at piano and play a group of two black keys (both keys at the same time). |

• Sing *If You're Happy and You Know It* without the CD. Instead of "clap your hands," everyone sings "play two keys," then plays a group of two black keys twice (tap, tap).

If you're happy and you know it, play two keys! (tap, tap)*
If you're happy and you know it, play two keys! (tap, tap)
If you're happy and you know it,
Then your face will surely show it,
If you're happy and you know it, play two keys! (tap, tap)

* Play group of two black keys two times.

| Teacher | Students |
|---|---|
| 10. Say: "You were so good at playing the groups of two black keys! Next, we will play a three-black-key group. Take fingers 2, 3 and 4 on your left hand and play a three-black-key group." The three black keys in each group can be played either individually or simultaneously. Take turns until all students have played. | 10. Play a group of three black keys with left hand using fingers 2, 3 and 4. |
| 11. Say: "Excellent! This time, I want you to take fingers 2, 3 and 4 on your right hand and play a three-black-key group." The three black keys in each group can be played either individually or simultaneously. Take turns until all students have played. | 11. Play a group of three black keys with right hand using fingers 2, 3 and 4. |
| 12. Say: "You sounded really good! We are going to sing *If You're Happy and You Know It* again. This time, we will say 'play three keys,' and we will play a group of three black keys, too (tap, tap)."<br><br>• Sing *If You're Happy and You Know It* without the CD. Instead of "clap your hands," everyone sings "play three keys," then plays a group of three black keys twice (tap, tap).<br><br>If you're happy and you know it, play three keys! (tap, tap)*<br>If you're happy and you know it, play three keys! (tap, tap)<br>If you're happy and you know it,<br>Then your face will surely show it,<br>If you're happy and you know it, play three keys! (tap, tap)<br><br><br>* Play group of three-black-keys two times. | 12. Stand at piano and play a group of three black keys (all three keys at the same time). |

## Part 2: Quarter Note Review

| Teacher | Students |
|---|---|
| 1. Say: "At our last lesson, we learned a song about Mozart Mouse. You were so good at singing this song and clapping a steady beat. Show me how you can do it again."<br><br>• Sing *Mozart Mouse's Song* (🎵 6) and clap. (See page 19 for lyrics.) | 1. Sit, sing, and clap. |
| 2. Ask: "Who remembers the name of the special note that is in this song?"<br><br>[Quarter note] | 2. Answer questions. |
| 3. Ask: "How many counts does a quarter note get?"<br><br>[One] | |
| 4. Say: "Great! I want you to do another page in your Music Workbook. Turn to page 9." Guide the student through the page according to the instructions in the student book. | 4. Sit and color page 9 in Music Workbook. |

| Teacher | Students |
|---|---|
| 1. Say, "The last time we read about our music friends Mozart Mouse and Beethoven Bear, they had just met a cat. Her name is Clara Schumann-Cat and she lives in the music store. (Show Clara Schumann-Cat plush animal.) She knows a lot about music, and she was going to give Mozart Mouse and Beethoven Bear piano lessons. I wonder what they are doing today." | 1. Sit and listen. |
| 2. Read the story aloud. | |

# Chapter 3: Loud and Soft Sounds

The next evening, Beethoven Bear and Mozart Mouse were waiting for the music store to close and Clara Schumann-Cat to arrive for their second piano lesson. Their first lesson the night before had been so much fun, but something very unusual had happened – or rather, had not happened. Mozart Mouse did not sneeze at all – not even once!

Beethoven Bear was thinking about that as they waited for Clara. "Mozart Mouse," he said, "I thought you were allergic to cats. Why weren't you sneezing last night?"

Mozart Mouse, who was sitting on the piano bench and looking at their piano book, paused for a moment and thought. "Hmm...I'm not sure," he finally said. "The only thing I can think of is that I must not be allergic to *musical* cats."

"That must be it!" Beethoven Bear agreed. Just then, he thought he heard a "tap, tap, tap" on the piano room door.

Mozart Mouse did not budge from the bench. "Did you hear that knocking sound?" Beethoven Bear asked. "I think Clara is here!"

"I didn't hear anything," Mozart Mouse replied as he turned another page. "Your ears must be playing tricks on you."

"Maybe so," said Beethoven Bear as he climbed onto the bench and sat next to Mozart Mouse. Just as he was getting ready to play, he heard another soft "tap, tap, tap."

"There it is again!" he exclaimed. "Did you hear it this time?"

Mozart Mouse's ears began to quiver. "I'm not sure. Let's both listen really carefully and see if it happens again."

This time, there was no mistaking it. There was a very loud "tap, tap, tap" at the door!

"That must be Clara!" Beethoven Bear cried, and the two music friends slid off the piano bench and raced to the door to greet her.

"Good evening," Clara purred, as she walked into the room.

"Hi, Clara," Mozart Mouse and Beethoven Bear said. "What are you going to teach us tonight?" Beethoven Bear asked excitedly.

"I actually have already started your lesson. Perhaps you noticed," Clara said with an air of mystery.

"What do you mean exactly?" Mozart Mouse asked.

Clara smiled and purred. "I knocked on the door three different times. The first two times were soft and the third time was loud."

Beethoven Bear shouted, "I knew it! I knew I heard you knocking!"

"But what does all that knocking have to do with playing the piano?" Mozart Mouse asked.

"Well," Clara answered. "Just as I was able to make soft and loud knocking sounds, I can make soft and loud sounds on the piano as well. Listen! Let me show you how."

The three hopped up onto the piano bench, and Clara opened up their music book. She turned to a page that had the letter "p" on it and began to explain.

"In music, we use Italian words to tell us how loud or soft we should play. The Italian word for soft is 'piano.' We use the letter 'p' in the music to tell us to play softly."

"What if we want to play loudly?" Mozart Mouse asked.

Clara answered by turning to another page. "Here is the letter 'f.' This stands for the Italian word 'forte' which means loud."

"This is so exciting!" Beethoven Bear exclaimed. "Now we can play our pieces with loud and soft sounds! I can't wait to try it."

"Me, too!" said Mozart Mouse, and they spent the rest of the evening playing the new loud and soft sounds they had learned.

## Part 4: Half Notes, Loud and Soft Sounds

| Teacher | Students |
|---|---|
| 1. Say: "Mozart Mouse and Beethoven Bear learned how to make loud and soft sounds on the piano. We have a song to sing that has loud and soft sounds in it. It is about our music friend, Beethoven Bear. We are going to listen and move to *Beethoven Bear's Song.*"<br><br>• Sing *Beethoven Bear's Song* (🎵 **8**). | 1. Stand and follow movements in song (march and tiptoe). |

| | |
|---|---|
| 2. Say: "That was fun! Did you hear some quarter notes in *Beethoven Bear's Song?* We sang some. But there is also a new note in the song. It is a longer note than a quarter note. It is called a half note. Open your Music Workbook to page 10. This is what a half note looks like. It is a long note. It gets two counts. Trace each half note with a black crayon. Color each '1–2' red." | 2. Trace half notes and color counts on page 10 in Music Workbook. |
| 3. "When we clap half notes, we keep a steady beat. Let's clap and count the half notes on this page." | 3. Sit, clap and count, saying "1-2" for each half note. |

| Teacher | Students |
|---|---|
| 4. Say: "Now we can clap the rhythm of Beethoven Bear's name! It uses a half note, two quarter notes and then a half note. It sounds like this: (clap and count)  Show: Clap and squeeze on "Bee" (rhymes with "bay"). Clap one time each on "tho" (rhymes with "toe") and "ven" (rhymes with "bin"). Then clap and squeeze on "Bear." It's your turn to clap and count." | 4. Clap and count 1–2, 1, 1, 1–2. |
| 5. "Very good! Let's stand and sing *Beethoven Bear's Song* one more time. When the music gets softer, I want you to keep singing but sit down." <br>• Sing *Beethoven Bear's Song* (🞉 **8**). | 5. Stand and sing. Sit down for the second verse. |
| 6. Say: "We have time to do one more page in our Music Workbook. Turn to page 11." Guide the student through the page according to the instructions in the student book. | 6. Sit and color page 11 in Music Workbook. |

## Part 5: Goodbye Song

| Teacher | Students |
|---|---|
| 1. Say: "You all were good listeners today! Beethoven Bear and Mozart Mouse learned about soft and loud sounds today and so did you. And you learned what a half note is and how many counts it gets. You played groups of two and three black keys on the piano, too. It is time to say goodbye, and sing the *Goodbye Song*." (See page 13 for lyrics.) <br>• Play *Goodbye Song* (🞉 **5**). | 1. Stand, sing, and imitate motions. |

# Lesson 4
## Fast and Slow

Musical Concept Emphasis:  Whole Note, Fast and Slow

## Teaching Materials

❑ *Meet the Music Friends* Curriculum Book and CD

❑ *Meet the Music Friends* Music Workbook for each student (pages 12-14)

❑ CD player

❑ Beethoven Bear, Mozart Mouse, and Clara Schumann-Cat plush animals

❑ Crayons for each student

page 12

page 13

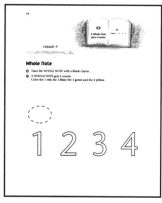

page 14

## Lesson 4 Overview

**Part 1:  Hello Song and Quarter Note Review**
- *Hello Song* (🔊 1)
- *Mozart Mouse's Song* (🔊 6)
- Review quarter note.
- Play Mozart Mouse's name on the keyboard (Music Workbook, page 13).

**Part 2:  Half Note Review**
- Review half note.
- *Beethoven Bear's Song* (🔊 8)
- Play Beethoven Bear's name on the keyboard (Music Workbook, page 12).

**Part 3:  Fast and Slow**
- Read story.
- *The Old Gray Cat* (🔊 9)

**Part 4:  Whole Notes**
- Introduce the whole note.
- Complete Music Workbook, page 14.
- *The Whole Note Song* (🔊 10)

**Part 5:  Goodbye Song**
- *Goodbye Song* (🔊 5)

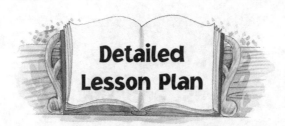

# Detailed Lesson Plan

## Part 1: Hello Song and Quarter Note Review

| Teacher | Students |
|---|---|
| 1. Sing *Hello Song* (💿 1) with the movements. (See page 5 for lyrics.) | 1. Stand, sing, and follow the teacher's movements. |
| 2. Say: "Your voices sound nice and strong today! Let's sing another song. Mozart Mouse would like us to sing and clap his special song."<br><br>• Sing *Mozart Mouse's Song* (💿 6) and clap. (See page 19 for lyrics.) | 2. Sit, sing, and clap. |
| 3. Ask: "Who remembers the name of the note that is in this piece?"<br><br>[Quarter note] | 3. Sit and answer questions. |
| 4. Ask: "How many counts does a quarter note get?"<br><br>[One] | |
| 5. Say: "Very good! Take out your Music Workbook and turn to page 13. We can play Mozart Mouse's name on the piano by following the notes on this page. The picture of the hand tells us which hand to use." | 5. Take out Music Workbook, turn to page 13, and answer questions. |
| 6. Say: "Hold up the hand that matches the picture. That is correct; it is the right hand." | |
| 7. Say: Ask: "Which group of black keys will we play?"<br><br>[Two] | |
| 8. "This number tells us which finger will play first" (point to fingering over first quarter note). | |
| 9. Ask: "Which finger will we start with? That is right—finger number 2."<br><br>[2] | |
| 10. Say: "Let's go to the piano to play this piece."<br><br>• Follow directions on the page. | 10. Line up at the piano and take turns playing Mozart Mouse's name. |

## Part 2: Half Note Review

| Teacher | Students |
|---|---|
| 1. Say: "You sounded terrific! Sit down on the floor. We learned a song about Beethoven Bear, too. It has a note we learned in our last class. Who can tell me the name of the new note?"<br><br>[Half note] | 1. Sit and answer questions. |
| 2. Ask: "How many counts does a half note get?"<br><br>[Two] | |
| 3. Say: "Great! This is how we clap and count a half note."<br><br>Show: Clap both hands on count "one" and keep them together. On count "two," squeeze your hands together and swing them down. | |
| 4. Say: "This is how we clap Beethoven Bear's name." (See page 28.) Demonstrate clapping Beethoven Bear's name. | |
| 5. Say: "Now you try it with me." (Repeat several times until the students are comfortable with the rhythm.) | 5. Clap and chant Bee-tho-ven Bear. |
| 6. Say: "We don't want Beethoven Bear to feel left out, so now we are going to sing his special song. When we hear his name, we are going to clap the rhythm of it."<br><br>• Sing *Beethoven Bear's Song* (💿 8). (See page 27 for lyrics.) | 6. Sing and clap rhythm for Beethoven Bear. |
| 7. Say: "That sounded great! Open your Music Workbook again, this time to page 12. We can play Beethoven Bear's name on the piano, too! Look at the page carefully." | 7. Take out Music Workbook, turn to page 12 and answer questions. |
| 8. Ask: "Who can tell me which hand we will use?"<br><br>[Left hand] | |
| 9. Ask: "Which black key group will we play?"<br><br>[Three] | |
| 10. Ask: "Which finger will we start with?"<br><br>[2] | |
| 11. Say: "Good! Let's go to the piano and play Beethoven Bear's name."<br><br>• Follow directions on the page. | 11. Line up at the piano and take turns playing Beethoven Bear's name. |

| Teacher | Students |
|---|---|
| 1. Say: "It is time for us to see what our music friends, Beethoven Bear and Mozart Mouse, are doing today. Do you think they will have another lesson with Clara Schumann-Cat? Listen to our story and find out!"<br>2. Read the story aloud. | 1. Sit and listen. |

# Chapter 4: Fast and Slow

Mozart Mouse and Beethoven Bear were discussing all of the things they had learned from the children's piano classes and from Clara Schumann-Cat. Mozart Mouse began the list. "We know high and low," he said. "And up and down," Beethoven Bear added.

Mozart Mouse continued, "We know our groups of two and three black keys."

"And don't forget that we know quarter and half notes, too!" Beethoven Bear reminded him. Then he asked Mozart Mouse a question. "What's your favorite song we have learned so far?"

Mozart Mouse thought for just a second. "Why, the song that has my name in it, of course—*Mozart Mouse's Song!* What about you? Which song do you like best?"

"That's easy!" Beethoven Bear exclaimed. "I like *Beethoven Bear's Song* best because it has my name in it, too!"

Then Beethoven Bear had another question. "I wonder if anyone has ever written a song for Clara Schumann-Cat?"

"We can ask her tonight!" Mozart Mouse exclaimed. "The music store is closed, and she should be here any minute."

It wasn't long until the music friends heard the familiar "tap-tap-tap" on the piano room door.

"Hi, Clara!" they cried as she walked into the room. "We have a question for you," Mozart Mouse announced. "Beethoven Bear and I were wondering if anyone has ever written a song about you?"

Clara Schumann-Cat purred with satisfaction. "Actually, I have had several songs written about me." She swished her tail excitedly.

"Will you teach them to us?" Beethoven Bear asked.

"I will someday," Clara promised. "But tonight, I have a song about another cat. It is about an old, grey cat. It will teach you something new about playing piano: we can play fast, and we can play slow."

"Oh! I've always wanted to play fast!" Beethoven Bear exclaimed.

"Then let's listen to the song and see what it is all about."

Clara Schumann-Cat took the music friends over to the CD player, and their lesson began.

| Teacher | Students |
|---|---|
| 3. Say: "I know just the song that Clara Schumann-Cat was talking about. It is called *The Old Gray Cat.* The words are about a sleeping cat and some playful mice.<br><br>• Listen to *The Old Gray Cat* (🌀 **9**). | 3. Sit and listen. |

The Old Gray Cat

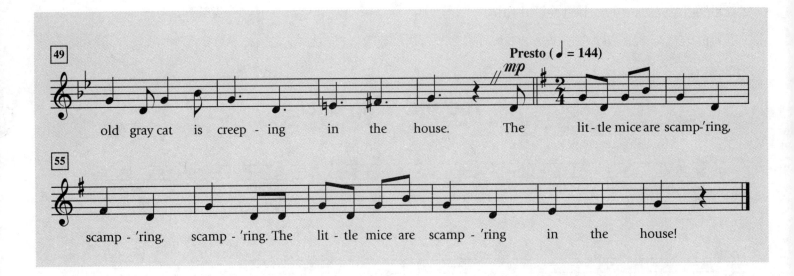

49 ... old gray cat is creep - ing in the house. The ... Presto (♩ = 144) *mp* ... lit - tle mice are scamp - 'ring,

55 ... scamp - 'ring, scamp - 'ring. The lit - tle mice are scamp - 'ring in the house!

| Teacher | Students |
|---|---|
| 4. Say: "We are going to listen to *The Old Gray Cat* again. This time, we will act out the story and sing along."<br><br>&bull; Some of the children are mice, and some are cats<br><br>&bull; Act out the story as the children sing. At the end of the song, everyone returns to his/her place on the floor.<br><br>5. Say: "In *The Old Gray Cat*, we heard some fast sounds and some slow sounds."<br><br>6. Ask: "What were the mice doing when the sounds were slow?"<br><br>[Creeping]<br><br>7. Ask: "What were the mice doing when the sounds were fast?"<br><br>[Scampering] | 4. Sing and act out story (sleep, creep, nibble, dance, scamper).<br><br><br><br><br><br>6. Sit and answer questions. |

## Part 4: Whole Notes

| Teacher | Students |
|---|---|
| 1. Say: "Open your Music Workbook to page 14. This is a new note. It is called a whole note. Whole notes last for a very long time. They get four counts like this: Clap on count 1; squeeze and shake on counts 2, 3, 4. Now, you try it with me."<br><br>&bull; Clap and count several whole notes.<br><br>"Now, trace the whole note on page 14 with a black crayon and color the counts with other colors." | 1. Clap and count whole notes, then color page 14 according to directions in the Music Workbook. |

## Part 4: Whole Notes

| Teacher | Students |
|---|---|
| 2. Say: "You clap whole notes really well! We have a new song to learn about whole notes. It is called *The Whole Note Song*. We are going to clap and count some whole notes during this song. Watch me, and I will show you when to clap and count."<br><br>• Play *The Whole Note Song* (🌐 **10**). | 2. Listen to song, clap and count whole notes as directed. |

## Part 5: Goodbye Song

| Teacher | Students |
|---|---|
| 1. Say: "You all were good listeners today!  Beethoven Bear and Mozart Mouse learned about fast and slow sounds today and so did you.  And you learned what a whole note is and how many counts it gets.  You played Mozart Mouse's and Beethoven Bear's names on the piano, too.  It is time to say goodbye and sing the *Goodbye Song*."  (See page 13 for lyrics.)<br><br>• Play *Goodbye Song* (🌀 **5**). | 1. Stand, sing, and imitate motions. |

# Lesson 5
## Review

Musical Concept Emphasis: Fast and Slow, Two and Three Black Keys,

Quarter Notes, Half Notes, Whole Notes

## Teaching Materials

❑ *Meet the Music Friends* Curriculum Book and CD

❑ *Meet the Music Friends* Music Workbook for each student (pages 15–16)

❑ CD player

❑ Beethoven Bear, Mozart Mouse, and Clara Schumann-Cat plush animals

❑ Crayons for each student

page 15

page 16

## Lesson 5 Overview

**Part 1:  Hello Song**

• *Hello Song* (🕪 **1**)

**Part 2:  The Recital**

• Read story.

**Part 3:  Review – Fast and Slow**

• *The Old Gray Cat* (🕪 **9**)

**Part 4:  Review – Two and Three Black Keys**

• *If You're Happy and You Know It* (🕪 **7**)

**Part 5:  Review – Quarter Notes**

• *Mozart Mouse's Song* (🕪 **6**)

• Play Mozart Mouse's name on the keyboard.

**Part 6:  Review – Half Notes**

• Play Beethoven Bear's name on the keyboard.

**Part 7:  Review – Whole Notes**

• *The Whole Note Song* (🕪 **10**)

• Clap rhythms in Music Workbook, page 15.

**Part 8:  Goodbye Song**

• *Goodbye Song* (🕪 **5**)

• Complete certificate in Music Workbook, page 16.

## Detailed Lesson Plan

### Part 1: Hello Song

| Teacher | Students |
|---|---|
| 1. Sing *Hello Song* (💿 **1**) with the movements. (See page 5 for lyrics.) | 1. Stand, sing, and follow the teacher's movements. |

### Part 2: The Recital

| Teacher | Students |
|---|---|
| 1. Say: "Mozart Mouse and Beethoven Bear are waiting for Clara to arrive for their piano lesson. Let's find out what they are doing." <br><br> 2. Read the story aloud. | 1. Sit and listen. |

## Chapter 5: The Music Friends' Recital

Mozart Mouse and Beethoven Bear were very busy preparing for their fifth piano lesson. They had decided that they wanted to surprise Clara Schumann-Cat by performing some of the pieces she had taught them!

Mozart Mouse was writing down the names of the pieces. "Help me decide which piece we should play first," said Mozart Mouse.

"I know!" Beethoven Bear exclaimed. "I think we should start with *If You're Happy and You Know It*. I just love playing the two and three black key groups!"

"That's a good idea," said Mozart Mouse as he wrote down the name of the piece. "Then

we should each play our name pieces. You can play yours first," Mozart Mouse offered graciously.

"Okay," Beethoven Bear agreed. "What about *The Whole Note Song*? Should we sing that for Clara?"

"Yes!" Mozart Mouse replied. "And I think we should end with *The Old Gray Cat*."

"Perfect!" Beethoven Bear said. "Should we decorate the program for Clara?"

"That would be fun!" Mozart Mouse answered as he handed Beethoven Bear some crayons. Together, they created a very beautiful program.

As they admired their work, Mozart Mouse said, "There is just one problem with it."

"What's wrong?" Beethoven Bear asked.

Mozart Mouse pointed to the top of the page. "I don't know what to put here. It needs a title. I don't know what you call a program of music. Do you?"

Beethoven Bear shook his head "no." "Let's ask Clara when she gets here," he suggested.

"But it will ruin her surprise!" Mozart Mouse said.

"I don't think she will suspect anything. I'll ask her, and when she tells us, you write it down on the paper," Beethoven Bear instructed.

As soon as he said that, they heard Clara's "tap-tap-tap" on the door.

"Good evening," Clara purred as she walked into the room. "Are you ready for your lesson to begin?" she asked.

"Yes," Beethoven Bear answered, "but before we begin, would you answer a question for us?"

"Of course!" Clara replied.

Beethoven Bear cleared his throat. "We were just wondering what you call a musical program where different pieces are performed."

"That's an excellent question," Clara purred proudly. "It's called a recital." As she answered, Mozart Mouse quickly wrote "Beethoven Bear and Mozart Mouse Present a Recital" on his paper. Clara did not see him!

Mozart Mouse walked over the where Clara and Beethoven Bear were sitting. He presented the paper to Clara with a grand bow.

"This is for you, Clara," he said. "Beethoven Bear and I have prepared a recital of our favorite pieces for you." (Mozart Mouse particularly liked saying the new word they had learned: recital.)

Beethoven Bear continued. "We would like you to relax and enjoy our program."

With that, Clara Schumann-Cat made herself comfortable. Mozart Mouse and Beethoven Bear had the most delightful time singing and playing their pieces for Clara. When they were finished, Clara was beaming with pride.

"Well done, my music friends, well done! You have been wonderful students, and you are fine performers. I hope this doesn't mean we are finished with our lessons together!" Her tail was swishing quickly as she spoke.

"No! " Beethoven Bear said. "Of course not!" Mozart Mouse agreed. "We just wanted to show you how much you have taught us already. It was our way of thanking you."

"Will you teach us some more?" Beethoven Bear asked.

"Absolutely!" Clara Schumann-Cat agreed. "Let's begin right away!"

And just like that, Mozart Mouse and Beethoven Bear started on the next part of their exciting music journey together beginning with the *Music for Little Mozarts* piano course.

**Note to Teacher:** Sections 3–7 review concepts learned during previous lessons. If there is not time in the lesson to review all of these sections, select the concepts that are most appropriate for your students.

## Part 3: Review: Fast and Slow

| Teacher | Students |
|---|---|
| 1. Say: "I need our cats and mice to come out and play now. We will sing *The Old Grey Cat*, and I would like for you to act out the story as you sing."<br><br>• Play *The Old Grey Cat* (🎵 **9**). (See page 33 for lyrics.)<br>• Some of the children are mice, and some are cats.<br>• Act out the story as the children sing. At the end of the song, everyone returns to his/her place on the floor. | 1. Sing and act out story. |

## Part 4: Review: Two and Three Black Keys

| Teacher | Students |
|---|---|
| 1. Say: "Good job! Get ready to clap your hands and sing *If You're Happy and You Know It*." (See page 23 for lyrics.)<br><br>• Play *If You're Happy and You Know It* (🎵 **7**) | 1. Stand up, sing, and clap. |
| 2. Say: "We'll sing it again, but this time, we will change the words. Instead of singing, 'If you're happy and you know it, clap your hands,' we are going to sing, 'If you're happy and you know it, play two keys.' Then, you will play two black keys with fingers 2 and 3 with either hand (tap, tap)." (See page 23 for lyrics. Sing and demonstrate.) | 2. Stand at piano and play a group of two black keys two times. |
| 3. Say: "You sounded really good! Let's sing *If You're Happy and You Know It* again. This time, we will say 'play three keys (tap, tap),' and we will play three black keys, too. You will use fingers 2, 3 and 4 with either hand." (See page 24 for lyrics.) | 3. Stand at piano and play a group of three black keys two times. |

# Part 5: Review—Quarter Notes

| Teacher | Students |
|---|---|
| 1. Ask: "Who remembers the song we sing about Mozart Mouse? What special note is in his song? [quarter note] Let's sing and clap quarter notes while we listen to *Mozart Mouse's Song*." (See page 19 for lyrics.)<br><br>• Sing *Mozart Mouse's Song* (💿 **6**) and clap. | 1. Sit, sing, and clap. |
| 2. Ask: "How many counts does a quarter note get?" [one] | 2. Sit and answer question. |
| 3. Say: "Very good! Let's go back to the piano. We learned how to play Mozart Mouse's name on the piano last week. Here is the music (Place Music Workbook, page 13, open on piano). First, we are going to clap the rhythm pattern. Remember, we say "1" for each quarter note." | 3. Stand at piano, clap, and count. |
| 4. Say: "Take your right hand, fingers 2 and 3, and put them up in the air. When I say 'ready, play,' you are going to play and say the finger numbers for Mozart Mouse's name. Here we go. One, two, ready, play." | 4. Hold right hand in the air and "play" while saying 3-3-2. |
| 5. Say: "Good job! Now, find a two black key group on the piano and place your right hand fingers 2 and 3 on it. When I say 'ready, play,' I want you to play the black keys and say the finger numbers. Here we go. One, two, ready, play." (Students can play individually. Continue until everyone has a turn.) | 5. Play two-black-key group on the piano with fingers 2, 3 while saying 3-3-2. |

# Part 6: Review—Half Notes

| Teacher | Students |
|---|---|
| 1. Say: "You played that really well! Mozart Mouse would be very proud of you! Beethoven Bear wants us to play his song now. Let's clap his name first. Remember, there is a half note in it." | 1. Sit, answer questions, clap and say "Beethoven Bear." |
| 2. Ask: "How many counts does a half note get?" [two] | |
| 3. Say: "Good. Let's clap and say Beethoven Bear's name. Listen for when I say 'ready, clap.' Here we go. One, two, ready, clap." (See page 28.) | |
| 4. Say: "You did it! Next, we are going to clap his name and count like this. I'll go first. (Clap and demonstrate: 1–2, 1, 1, 1–2) Now we'll clap it together. Wait until you hear, 'ready, clap.' Here we go. One, two, ready, clap." | |
| 5. Say: "You are ready to play Beethoven's name! Come to the piano and look at page 12 in the Music Workbook. What hand do we use? [left] What group of black keys do we play? [three] And which fingers do we use?" [2, 3, 4] | 5. Stand at piano and answer questions. |

| Teacher | Students |
|---|---|
| 6. Say: "Very good! Before we play Beethoven's name on the piano, we need to play it in the air. Put your left hand in the air. Play and name the finger numbers with me. Listen for 'ready, play.' Here we go. One, two, ready, play. 2__, 3, 3, 4__." | 6. Hold left hand in the air and "play" while saying 2-3-3-4. |
| 7. Say: "You did it! Let's try it on the piano now. Find a group of three black keys with your left hand and put fingers 2, 3 and 4 on the keys. Now we are going to play and count. Here we go. One, two, ready, play. 2__, 3, 3, 4__." (Students can play individually. Continue until everyone has a turn.) | 7. Play three-black-key group on the piano with fingers 2, 3, 4 while saying 2-3-3-4. |

## Part 7: Review—Whole Notes

| Teacher | Students |
|---|---|
| 1. Say: "Wow! You sounded great! I want to sing another song, so take a seat on the floor. At our last lesson, we sang a song that has whole notes in it. Here is what a whole note looks like. (Show page 14 in the Music Workbook.) How many counts does a whole note get? [four] Listen to *The Whole Note Song*. Watch me, and I will show you when to clap and count the whole notes." (See page 35 for lyrics.)<br><br>• Play *The Whole Note Song* (💿 **10**). | 1. Sit, listen to song, answer question, clap and count whole notes as directed. |
| 2. Say: "Good job! Let's clap some more whole notes. Open your Music Workbook to page 15. There are two patterns on this page. These are called rhythm patterns. Point to the first one. Let's name each note in the pattern." | 2. Point to and name each note in the first pattern on page 15 of Music Workbook. |
| 3. Say: "Very good! Now, we are going to clap and count the first pattern." | 3. Clap and count. |
| 4. Say: "I like how well you counted! Look at the second rhythm pattern. Point to it. Now we will name each note in the pattern." | 4. Point to and name each note in the second pattern on page 15 of Music Workbook. |
| 5. Say: "That was correct! You are ready to clap and count this pattern." | 5. Clap and count. |

## Part 8: Goodbye Song

| Teacher | Students |
|---|---|
| 1. "It is time for us to say goodbye. You have learned so much in your five classes, and I have enjoyed teaching you! Your musical journey can continue. Just like Mozart Mouse and Beethoven Bear, you can take piano lessons, too. When you enroll in *Music for Little Mozarts* piano classes, you will learn to play the piano along with Mozart Mouse and Beethoven Bear. I hope to see you in those classes! Let's stand and sing the *Goodbye Song.*" (See page 13 for lyrics.)<br><br>• Play *Goodbye Song* (🛇 **5**).<br><br>2. Fill out certificate in Music Workbook, page 16 and congratulate each student. | 1. Stand, sing, and imitate motions. |